USBORNE

Middle Ages
Picture Book

Dr. Abigail Wheatley

Illustrated by Maria Royse

Designed by Stephen Moncrieff & Samantha Barrett

CONTENTS

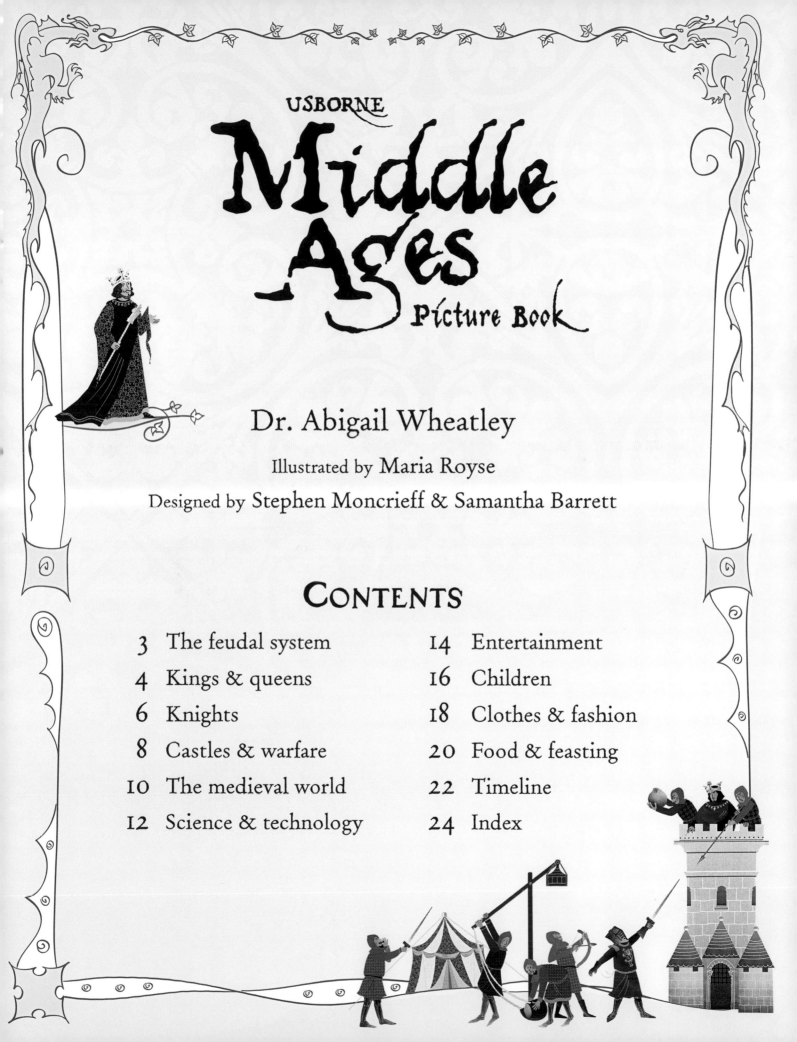

This is a medieval painting (meaning it's from the Middle Ages). It shows a fierce battle, with knights on horseback attacking each other. It was made around the year 1250 as an illustration for a book. At this time, all books were written out and illustrated by hand.

The Middle Ages was a period in European history around 1,000 to 500 years ago. It was a turbulent time of terrible wars, bitter religious conflicts and dreadful diseases. But, despite this, people had a great love of life, which they expressed in flamboyant fashions, magnificent feasts and joyful celebrations.

THE FEUDAL SYSTEM

During the Middle Ages, many countries were run according to the feudal system. This meant that a king owned the land, but loaned parts to his followers. They loaned parts to their followers, and so on.

The King owned all the land. He kept some, and granted some to great noblemen – leading lords and churchmen.

In return for their land, the great noblemen promised to fight for the king for a certain number of days a year. They granted some of their land to knights.

In return for their land, the knights promised to fight for the great noblemen. They granted some of their land to peasants, who lived and farmed there.

The peasants usually paid the knights rent. Many of them also had to promise to work for the knights, farming their land.

But there were always some people who didn't really fit into the feudal system...

Some knights didn't want to fight for their lord. They paid him instead.

Some women made a living from business or property.

Merchants and craftworkers earned money by making or selling things.

Some churchmen lived by collecting a share of goods people made, crops they grew or money they earned.

KINGS & QUEENS

In the Middle Ages, kings and queens ran their countries, led their armies in wars and owned vast areas of land. Their glittering crowns and rich robes showed everyone how powerful they were.

This splendid cloak was made for King Roger II of Sicily (now part of Italy) around 1133. It's made from red silk, gold thread and pearls.

When a medieval king led his troops into battle, he often wore a crown around his helmet, so everyone could see who he was.

A ceremony known as a coronation was an important part of becoming a king or queen. During the ceremony it was traditional for a leading churchman to put a crown on the monarch's head.

Kings and queens sat on elaborate chairs during coronation ceremonies. This one dates from 1296 and is still used during British coronations.

Crowns came in many shapes and sizes. In fact, kings and queens often had different crowns for different occasions. The ones here were all used for coronations.

This crown may date from around the year 700. It first belonged to the kings of Lombardy, a region of Italy. Later, it was used to crown kings of all Italy.

This gold crown is thought to date from around 1000, when the first King of Hungary was crowned.

This crown is part of the Bohemian Crown Jewels. It's made of gold, decorated with pearls, rubies, emeralds, and sapphires. Czech king Charles IV was the first to use it for his coronation in 1347.

As well as a crown to wear, every king or queen had a golden ball and rod to hold.

The ball was known as an orb. The round part represented the world, while the cross symbolized the Christian faith. This orb is encrusted with jewels.

A king or queen held the rod and ball for important occasions including ceremonies such as coronations.

A king or queen had the power to make laws. This painting shows a queen holding a legal document.

KNIGHTS

Knights were noblemen trained from a young age to fight fearlessly, even in the face of death. They were also supposed to be loyal and selfless, and protect those weaker than themselves.

Knights often took inspiration from legendary figures such as St. George, who defeated an evil dragon.

JOUSTS

As well as fighting real battles, knights also took part in jousts – mock fights where they tried to knock each other off their horses in front of crowds of cheering spectators.

BATTLE GEAR

Knights wore metal suits to protect them. Some parts were made from shiny metal sheets; others were made from linked metal rings, known as chain mail.

Suits like this, made of metal sheets strapped over chain mail, were worn around 1350.

This style of suit dates from around 1200. Only the helmet is solid metal.

This style of suit was worn around 1450. Almost all of it is made from sheets of metal.

LADIES

Knights were supposed to respect and protect all ladies. It was thought that love between a knight and his chosen lady would inspire the knight to do brave and noble deeds in battle.

This precious ornament was probably given by a knight to the lady he wanted to marry. It's made from gold, enamel, pearls and jewels.

BECOMING A KNIGHT

To become a knight, a man had to go through an elaborate ceremony during which a king or great lord gave him weapons and declared he was a knight.

COATS OF ARMS

Each family of knights had its own distinctive badge, known as a coat of arms. Originally, knights displayed these on their shields, but later they blazoned them proudly on buildings, furnishings and clothing.

Coats of arms could show patterns or pictures, or a combination of both.

This royal coat of arms, made from painted and gilded stone, was used to decorate a building.

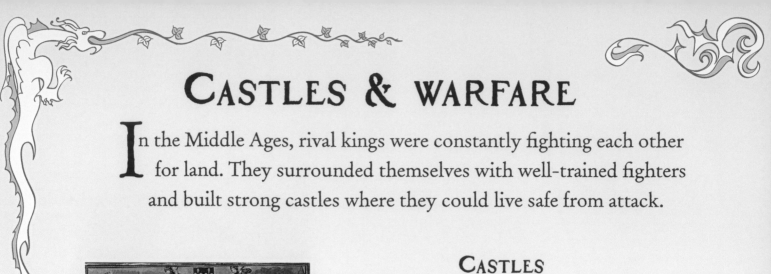

CASTLES & WARFARE

In the Middle Ages, rival kings were constantly fighting each other for land. They surrounded themselves with well-trained fighters and built strong castles where they could live safe from attack.

CASTLES

Every lord had at least one castle defended by deep ditches and thick walls crowned with tall towers. But this didn't stop rival lords from attacking, using a variety of weapons.

High walls weren't always enough to keep out enemies. This medieval painting shows soldiers swarming up ladders, to get over the walls.

Machines called trebuchets were used to throw rocks, to try to smash through castle walls.

Some trebuchets were small, but this is a huge one, powered by a heavy weight and capable of flinging massive rocks.

This is a medieval illustration of an early gun. At first, around 1270, guns were fairly weak and unreliable. But, by around 1420 there were stronger guns that could smash castle walls to pieces.

WEAPONS

Knights and soldiers used a variety of fearsome weapons against one another. Here are just some of them.

This spiked flail was used to crush and dent enemies' helmets and metal suits.

Battle-axes, like this one, were used in hand-to-hand fighting, but could also be thrown at enemies.

This magnificent sword was made around 900 years ago. Next to it is its jewel-studded carrying case, or scabbard.

During battles, knights on horseback charged headlong at each other, wielding spears, battle-axes or drawn swords.

STEEDS

War horses, or steeds, were a knight's most expensive and valued possession, and an essential part of any medieval army.

During battles, some steeds wore a covering of protective metal plates. This one is beautifully decorated.

This is a spur. It was attached to a knight's foot to encourage his steed to go faster.

THE MEDIEVAL WORLD

Across much of Europe and around the Mediterranean, people shared a fairly similar way of life. Bad roads and wars made travel difficult, but some people still made long voyages, spreading new ideas and fashions as they went.

Sea voyages involved many hazards, including storms, shipwrecks and pirates. Many ships were well armed, to keep pirates at bay.

The Kings of England kept on trying to conquer Wales, Scotland and Ireland. Fighting was fierce.

Bannockburn ✕

Clontarf ✕

LUBECK ◉
HAMBURG ◉

ANTWERP ◉
GHENT ◉   COLOGNE ◉
LONDON ◉
Hastings ✕   BRUSSELS ◉
Agincourt ✕ ✕ Bouvines
MAINZ ◉

Cologne was famous for its great cathedral. Begun in 1248, it took 600 years to complete.

PARIS ◉

ORLEANS ◉   STRASBOURG ◉

✕ Lechfeld
✕ Morgarten

In southern France there were vast forests where noblemen could hunt deer and other wild animals.

MILAN ◉   VENICE ◉

AVIGNON ◉   GENOA ◉   BOLOGNA ◉

FLORENCE ◉

Bologna was well known for its university. Founded in 1088, it was the first in Europe.

ROME ◉

For much of the period, Spain and Portugal were divided into areas ruled by Christian and Muslim kings, who fought one another.

BARCELONA ◉

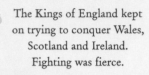

◉ TOLEDO

✕ Las Navas de Tolosa

CORDOBA ◉

SEVILLE ◉   ◉ GRANADA

PALERMO ◉

TUNIS ◉

MAP KEY

Wealthy city ◉
Famous battle ✕

Neva ✕

Novgorod was a wealthy trading city, exporting huge numbers of furs from animals hunted nearby.

PSKOV ◉

◉ NOVGOROD

TVER ◉

◉ RIGA

MOSCOW ◉

◉ SMOLENSK

✕ Grunwald

Roads were often clogged with mud or dust. Only rich ladies rode in fine carriages like this one. Most people went on horseback, or trudged along on foot.

Armies from Eastern Europe often had to fight off powerful invaders from central Asia.

◉ BELGRADE ✕
Nicopolis

Kosovo
✕

CONSTANTINOPLE ◉
(now Istanbul)

ATHENS ◉

ANTIOCH ◉

◉ ALEPPO

TRIPOLI ◉

◉ DAMASCUS

TYRE ◉
ACRE ◉ ✕ Hattin

◉ JERUSALEM

MEDIEVAL MAPS

Most medieval maps were far from accurate - but then they weren't designed to help people find their way. Instead they gave an overview of the world, with its amazing diversity of places, history, animals and other marvels.

This is a copy of a medieval world map. The countries of the world are shown squashed up to fit within a circle. Their shapes aren't easy to recognize today.

At the edges of maps there were often pictures of strange monsters like these, that were thought to live in far-away places.

The area around Jerusalem was known as the Holy Land. It was the scene of many battles between Christians and Muslims, who both wanted to control the area.

Science & Technology

Medieval people didn't know about scientific ideas we take for granted. But they were at the cutting edge of technology in areas such as stonework, and developed a number of clever inventions.

Using basic tools, medieval builders constructed some of the most impressive stone buildings ever made, from soaring cathedrals to magnificent castles.

This is a page from a medieval notebook showing techniques builders used to measure stone when constructing towers and arches.

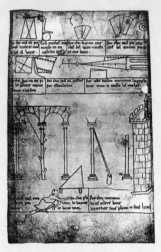

Star-gazing

Medieval Europeans learned about the stars and planets from books and instruments developed by scholars who lived in the Middle East and spoke Arabic languages.

This illustration from a medieval book shows a scholar studying the stars. He is holding a metal model showing the planets and the way they move.

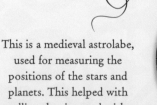

This is a medieval astrolabe, used for measuring the positions of the stars and planets. This helped with telling the time and with navigating during journeys by land or sea.

CLOCKS

In the early Middle Ages, clocks were powered by dripping water. But by around the year 1300, hanging weights were being used instead. This marked the beginning of modern clockwork.

This medieval painting shows a monk named Richard of Wallingford. He designed a clock that could tell the time and show the position of the Sun, moon and planets.

This face belongs to a clock made around 1390. The outer ring is marked into 24 hours, the middle ring shows minutes and the inner ring shows days of the month.

METALWORK

Some medieval skills were so advanced that modern technology can't do better. One example was bell-making, using melted metal. The technique has barely changed from the Middle Ages to today.

This medieval bell was cast from solid metal. Bells like this were hung in high towers so they could be heard from far and wide.

Medieval bell-makers at work

LENSES

These are the broken frames of some medieval spectacles, which held shaped glass lenses.

Spectacles for reading date from as early as 1268. They were difficult to make, so were very rare and expensive.

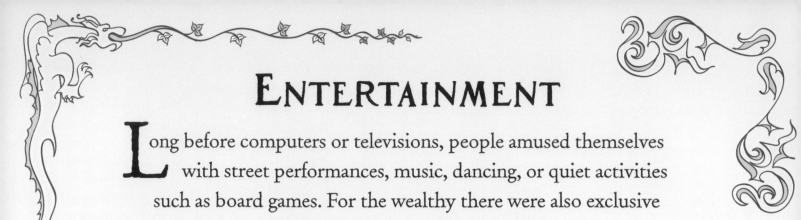

ENTERTAINMENT

Long before computers or televisions, people amused themselves with street performances, music, dancing, or quiet activities such as board games. For the wealthy there were also exclusive outdoor pursuits such as hunting.

PERFORMANCES

Plays were put on in the streets, on wagons fitted with scenery. The wagon stopped while people standing on it performed stories from the Bible. There were puppet shows, too.

This is a Nativity play, telling the story of the birth of the baby Jesus.

This hollow metal head probably comes from a puppet made around the year 1200.

MUSIC AND DANCING

Music was an important part of religious services and royal ceremonies. But it was also a part of celebrations for ordinary people. There were traditional tunes, often with accompanying words and dance steps, that people followed in particular regions, or for certain occasions.

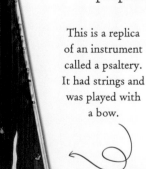

This is a replica of an instrument called a psaltery. It had strings and was played with a bow.

This is a replica crumhorn. To play it, you blew into the straight end and covered holes with your fingers, like playing a recorder.

Hunting and hawking

Hunting was a sport exclusively for royalty and nobles. They rode out with packs of hunting dogs to chase deer, wild boars, bears or other animals. Hawking was a type of hunting using trained birds of prey.

Hunting horns were used so that all the hunting party could keep in touch with one another, even in dense forest.

Huntsmen ran alongside the nobles to take care of the dogs.

In hawking, birds of prey were taught to catch small animals such as hares, and other birds such as herons and ducks. It took many months to train them, so they became very valuable.

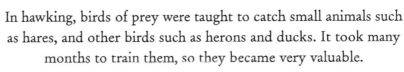

This carved ivory mirror back shows a noble couple going hawking. Their hawks are perched on their hands.

Playing games

Games involving boards, counters and dice were popular. Some people disapproved of dice games, if they involved gambling or cheating. But board games, especially chess, were considered perfectly respectable.

These chesspieces are in the shape of a foot soldier, a bishop and a knight. They were carved from walrus tusks around 1150-1200.

This medieval painting shows a couple playing a board game a little like backgammon.

CHILDREN

In the Middle Ages, children from ordinary families had to work for a living. Schools were rare, and only some wealthier children were taught how to read and write.

Country children helped their parents to grow and gather food.

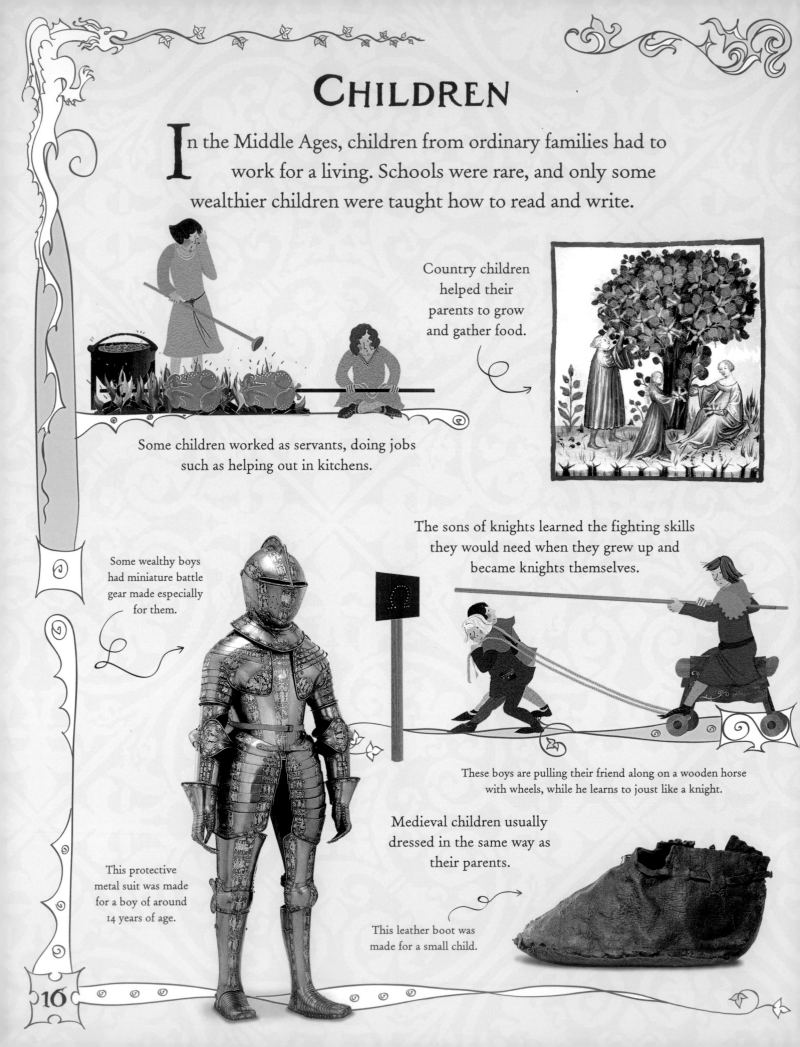

Some children worked as servants, doing jobs such as helping out in kitchens.

The sons of knights learned the fighting skills they would need when they grew up and became knights themselves.

Some wealthy boys had miniature battle gear made especially for them.

These boys are pulling their friend along on a wooden horse with wheels, while he learns to joust like a knight.

Medieval children usually dressed in the same way as their parents.

This protective metal suit was made for a boy of around 14 years of age.

This leather boot was made for a small child.

Toys and Games

Children's toys ranged from stilts and spinning tops to dolls, miniature kitchen equipment and model knights and castles.

These children are playing on wooden stilts.

This carved and painted wooden doll was made in Germany around 1530. Most dolls were much rougher, homemade creations.

This is a little toy jug. Children also had tiny cups and plates to play with.

This toy knight on a horse is made from hollow metal and dates from around 1300.

Reading and Writing

Most schools were strictly reserved for boys who were training to become priests or monks. Some parents or employers taught the children in their care, while wealthy parents might pay a tutor to teach their children.

This elaborate child's silver bowl is decorated with the letters of the alphabet.

It was probably made for a wealthy child to eat from, and learn from at the same time.

These children are learning to read from books, with the help of their tutor.

Clothes & Fashion

In the Middle Ages, your clothes told everyone who you were. Laws set out that ordinary people must wear plain, rough garments, while lords and ladies could wear silks, furs and jewels.

All clothes were hand-sewn. Many people made their own, while the better-off paid tailors to sew their clothes for them.

If you couldn't afford new clothes or shoes, you could buy used ones.

This painting from a medieval book shows a wealthy man trying on a stylish blue coat that a tailor is making for him.

These leather shoes reflect changing fashions in medieval times.

This slip-on shoe with leaf patterns dates from around 1400.

This very pointed style was fashionable around 1380. The point was stiffened by stuffing it with moss or hair.

Made soon after 1200, this shoe has decorative holes cut into it.

This gold and enamel swan badge was probably given by a lord to one of his wealthy supporters. It's just 3cm (1 inch) high.

Badges

Lords often gave their servants and supporters uniforms or badges to wear, to match their coat of arms (see page 7).

ACCESSORIES

You could buy all sorts of accessories such as belts, ribbons, gloves and purses from shops or markets, or from pedlars, who were salesmen who took their goods from place to place to sell them.

This pedlar is showing belts and purses to a lady customer. You can see the donkey he uses to carry his goods around.

This medieval coin purse is made from embroidered cloth and decorated with tassels. It would have been worn attached to a belt.

This is part of a belt that once belonged to a very wealthy man. It's made from silver decorated with gold, emeralds, pearls, crystal and enamel.

HAIR STYLES

Married women and nuns often covered their hair as a sign of modesty. Elaborate braided hairstyles were also popular, whether they were on display or worn under a covering.

This medieval painting shows a maid wearing a head covering. She is helping a wealthy lady to braid her hair.

The maid is holding up a round mirror so her mistress can see into it. On the lady's lap is a hair comb.

This delicate hair comb is carved from ivory. Less expensive combs were made from wood or bone.

Food & Feasting

What you ate depended on who you were. Ordinary people lived mostly on rough bread and vegetables. Wealthier people had meat and white bread, while lords ate expensive spiced dishes and sugary treats.

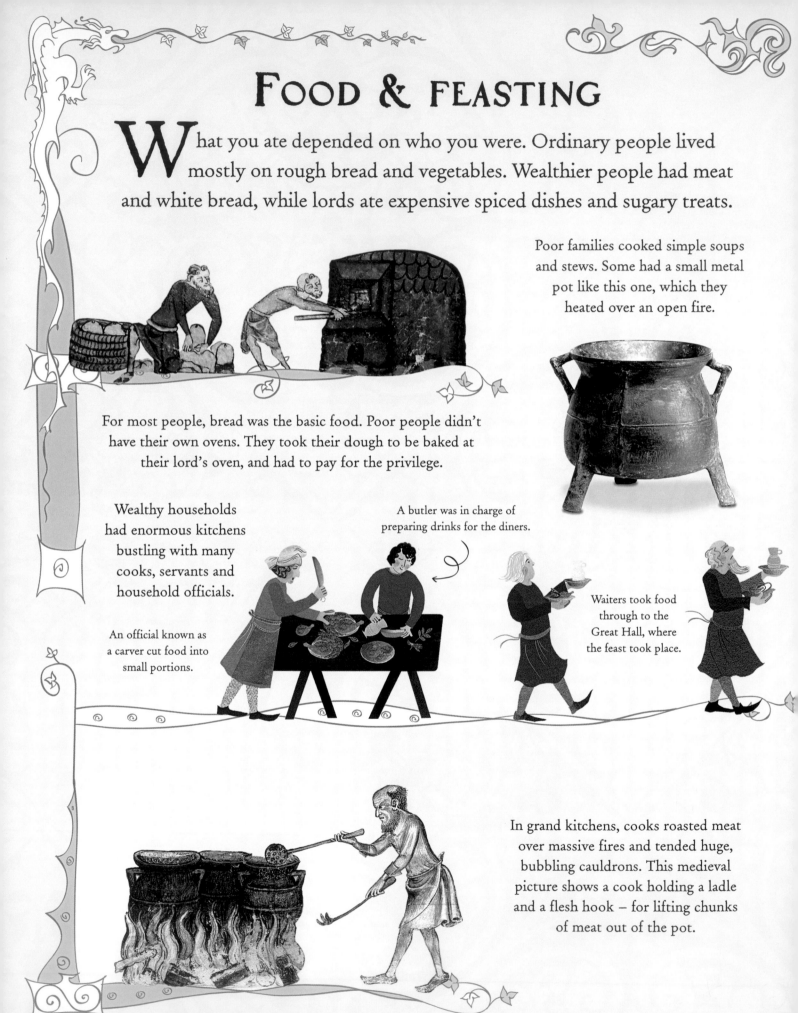

Poor families cooked simple soups and stews. Some had a small metal pot like this one, which they heated over an open fire.

For most people, bread was the basic food. Poor people didn't have their own ovens. They took their dough to be baked at their lord's oven, and had to pay for the privilege.

Wealthy households had enormous kitchens bustling with many cooks, servants and household officials.

A butler was in charge of preparing drinks for the diners.

An official known as a carver cut food into small portions.

Waiters took food through to the Great Hall, where the feast took place.

In grand kitchens, cooks roasted meat over massive fires and tended huge, bubbling cauldrons. This medieval picture shows a cook holding a ladle and a flesh hook – for lifting chunks of meat out of the pot.

Ordinary people ate using wooden spoons, bowls and cups, and served their drinks in pottery jugs.

This pottery jug dates from around the year 1500.

Poorer people often just grabbed a quick bite to eat where they worked. These farm workers have stopped for a lunch of bread and ale.

Wealthy merchants, churchmen and knights and ladies dined in grand style.

The most important diners ate at a table known as the high table, which stood on a raised platform.

A cupbearer carried wine and ale to the diners.

A marshal was in charge of serving the food, and made sure it was done very politely.

Wealthy diners carried their own fine spoons and knives with them. This spoon is made from gold and silver, decorated with enamel.

Elaborate containers, like this one, were put on the table at feasts. They were used to collect unused food, to give to the poor.

TIMELINE

This timeline shows just some of the most important things that happened in Europe during the Middle Ages. You'll find the battles marked on the map on pages 10–11.

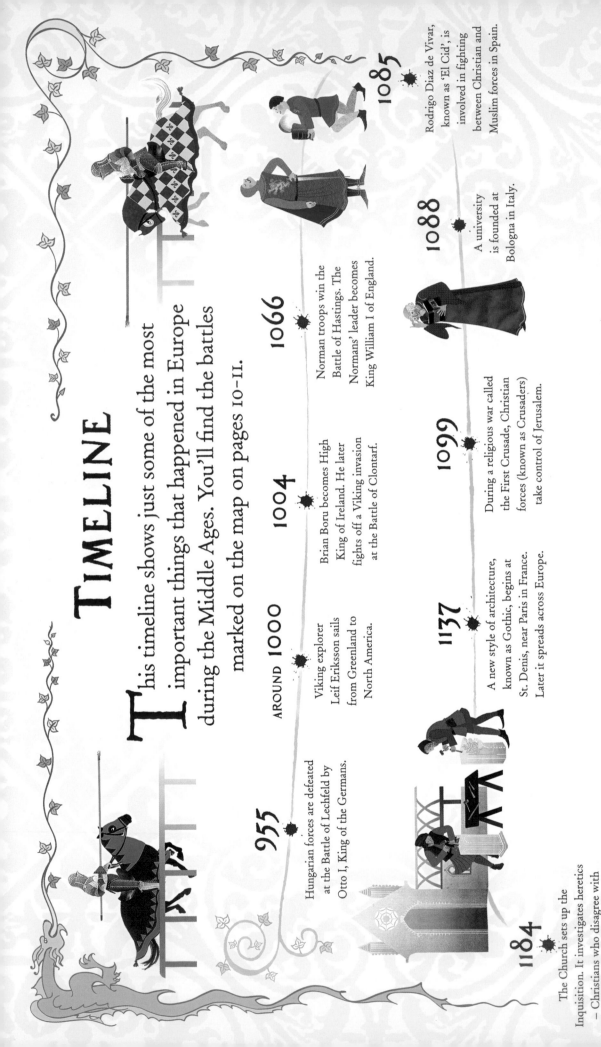

955
Hungarian forces are defeated at the Battle of Lechfeld by Otto I, King of the Germans.

AROUND 1000
Viking explorer Leif Eriksson sails from Greenland to North America.

1004
Brian Boru becomes High King of Ireland. He later fights off a Viking invasion at the Battle of Clontarf.

1066
Norman troops win the Battle of Hastings. The Normans' leader becomes King William I of England.

1085
Rodrigo Díaz de Vivar, known as 'El Cid', is involved in fighting between Christian and Muslim forces in Spain.

1088
A university is founded at Bologna in Italy.

1099
During a religious war called the First Crusade, Christian forces (known as Crusaders) take control of Jerusalem.

1137
A new style of architecture, known as Gothic, begins at St. Denis, near Paris in France. Later it spreads across Europe.

1184
The Church sets up the Inquisition. It investigates heretics – Christians who disagree with official Church teachings.

1187
Muslim leader Salah al-Din Yusuf ibn Ayyub (known as Saladin) defeats Crusaders at the Battle of Hattin.

1212
Spanish and Portuguese forces defeat the Muslim army of Caliph al-Nasir at the Battle of Las Navas de Tolosa.

1214
At the Battle of Bouvines the French drive the English out of all parts of France except for Gascony and Guyenne.

1240
The republic of Novgorod, led by Alexander 'Nevsky', defeats an invasion by Swedish, Norwegian and Finnish troops at the Battle of the Neva.

1265
The great poet Dante Alighieri is born in Florence, Italy.

1290
All Jewish people living in England are forced to become Christians or leave the country.

1295
Marco Polo, an Italian merchant, publishes tales of his travels to Asia, and as far as China.

1309
The Pope moves to Avignon in southern France, as part of a split within the Church, known as the Great Schism.

1314
Scots forces led by Robert the Bruce defeat the English army at the Battle of Bannockburn.

1315
At the Battle of Morgarten, Swiss peasants fight off an army led by Leopold I of Austria.

1337
A war begins between France and England that lasts until 1453. It becomes known as the Hundred Years War.

AROUND 1345
Geoffrey Chaucer, a great English poet, is born.

1346
Charles IV becomes King of Bohemia. A golden age begins for Bohemia and its capital city, Prague.

1347
A terrible plague known as the Black Death arrives in Europe. Eventually it kills one in three people.

AROUND 1350
The first guns are used in Europe. They are big, unreliable and inaccurate, but soon become more deadly.

1358
Peasants in northern France rise up in protest at harsh taxes and other duties, in a revolt known as the Jacquerie. It is quickly suppressed.

1389
At the Battle of Kosovo, Serbian and Bosnian forces are defeated by the Ottoman Turks, from central Asia.

1396
Ottoman forces defeat an army of Europeans at the Battle of Nicopolis.

1407
The first European public bank is established in Genoa, Italy.

1410
Polish and Lithuanian troops win the Battle of Grunwald, defeating Crusaders known as the Teutonic Knights.

1415
English forces defeat superior numbers of French at the Battle of Agincourt.

1429
A peasant girl called Joan of Arc helps French forces fighting the English. She is later burned as a witch.

1452
Great artist and inventor Leonardo da Vinci is born near Florence in Italy.

Index

Usborne Quicklinks

For links to websites where you can find out more about the Middle Ages, go to **www.usborne.com/quicklinks** and type in the keywords **Middle Ages Picture Book**. Please read our internet safety guidelines at the Usborne Quicklinks website. We recommend that children are supervised while using the internet.

Acknowledgements

Every effort has been made to trace and acknowledge ownership of copyright. If any rights have been omitted, the publishers offer to rectify this in any future editions following notification. The publishers are grateful to the following individuals and organizations for their permission to reproduce material on the following pages:

Cover: t The Annunciation with two saints and four prophets, 1333 (tempera on panel), Martini, Simone (1284-1344) & Memmi, Lippo (fl.1317-47) / Galleria degli Uffizi, Florence, Italy / Giraudon / The Bridgeman Art Library; l Suit of armour thought to have belonged to Chevalier Bayard (1475-1524), c.1510 (metal), Italian School, (16th century) / Musée de l'Armée, Paris, France / Giraudon / The Bridgeman Art Library; b Fascimile of September: harvesting grapes by the Limbourg brothers, from the 'Tres Riches Heures du Duc de Berry' (vellum) (for original see 8441), French School, (15th century) (after) / Victoria & Albert Museum, London, UK / The Bridgeman Art Library.

p2-3 The Middle Ages: p2 Ms M 638 f.10v Joshua, from the Morgan Picture Bible, c.1244-54 (vellum), French School, (13th century) / Pierpont Morgan Library, New York, USA / The Bridgeman Art Library.

p4-5 Kings & queens: p4t akg-images / Erich Lessing; p4bl © The Print Collector / Alamy; p4br © Hoberman Collection / Alamy; p5tr © The Bridgeman Art Library Ltd. / Alamy; p5tm © Interfoto / Alamy; p5ml © Petr Bonek / Alamy; p5bm akg-images; p5br © The British Library Board, Cotton Nero D. VII, f.7.

p6-7 Knights: p6bl Model of a man at arms in Italian armour of the late 13th century (mixed media), Wroe, Peter (20th century) / Royal Armouries, Leeds, UK / The Bridgeman Art Library; p6bm Model of a man at arms in Italian armour of the late 14th century (mixed media), Wroe, Peter (20th century) / Royal Armouries, Leeds, UK / The Bridgeman Art Library; p6br © Royal Armouries, II.194; p7t KHM-Museumsverband / Kunsthistorisches Museum Vienna; p7m © The British Library Board, Add. 10292, f.151v; p7b © Museum of London.

p8-9 Castles & warfare: p8t © The British Library Board, Royal 20 C. IX, f.156v; p8bl © Hemis / Alamy; p8br akg-images / Erich Lessing; p9tl akg-images / Erich Lessing; p9tm Ronald Sheridan/Ancient Art & Architecture Collection Ltd.; p9tr © INTERFOTO / Alamy; p9bl © Paris - Musée de l'Armée, Dist. RMN-Grand Palais / Emilie Cambier; p9br Horse armour of King Henry VIII, known as the Burgundian Bard, c.1511-15 (metal), Margot, Guille (fl.c.1515) / Royal Armouries, Leeds, UK / The Bridgeman Art Library.

p10-11 The medieval world: p11tr Facsimile copy of the 'Ebstorf Mappamundi', originally made for the convent at Ebstorf, near Luneberg, c.1339 but destroyed in 1943 (colour litho), . / British Library, London, UK / © British Library Board. All Rights Reserved / The Bridgeman Art Library.

p12-13 Science & technology: p12tr Ms.Fr.19093 fol.20v Geometrical figures for construction, arches and man measuring the height of a tower (facsimile copy) (pen & ink on paper) (b/w photo), Villard de Honnecourt (fl.1190-1235) / Bibliothèque Nationale, Paris, France / Giraudon / The Bridgeman Art Library; p12bl © The Bridgeman Art Library Ltd. / Alamy; p12br © The Trustees of the British Museum; p13tl © The British Library Board, Cotton Claudius E IV, f.201; p13tr © travelib history / Alamy; p13m © photoneye / shutterstock; p13b © Museum of London.

p14-15 Entertainment: p14tr © Museum of London; p14bl © Lebrecht Music and Arts Photo Library / Alamy; p14br © INTERFOTO / Alamy; p15t © The Trustees of the British Museum; p15m © The Trustees of the British Museum; p15bl © Peter Barritt / Alamy; p15br © The British Library Board, Add. 42130, f.76v.

p16-17 Children: p16tr © PRISMA ARCHIVO / Alamy; p16bl Boy's armour, probably made for Henry, Prince of Wales, c.1608 (metal), Dutch School, (17th century) / Royal Armouries, Leeds, UK / The Bridgeman Art Library; p16br © Museum of London; p17tr Germanisches Nationalmuseum, Nürnberg Foto: M Runge; p17ml © Museum of London; p17m © Museum of London; p17bl Copyright © Victoria and Albert Museum, London / V&A Images -- All rights reserved.

p18-19 Clothes & fashion: p18tl © PRISMA ARCHIVO / Alamy; p18m © Museum of London; p18br © The Trustees of the British Museum; p19tr akg-images / Interfoto; p19m Girdle made from three types of decorative plaques linked by hinges, European, c.1350-1400 (silver gilt, enamel. rock crystal and pearls) (detail of 307597), . / © Courtesy of the Warden and Scholars of New College, Oxford / The Bridgeman Art Library; p19bl © The British Library Board, Add. 42130, f.63; p19br Copyright © Victoria and Albert Museum, London / V&A Images -- All rights reserved.

p20-21 Food & feasting: p20tl © The British Library Board, Royal 10 E IV, f.145v; p20tr © Museum of London; p20b © The British Library Board, Add. 42130, f.207; p21tl © BnF, Dist. RMN-Grand Palais / image BnF; p21tr © Museum of London; p21bl © The Trustees of the British Museum; p21br Copyright © Victoria and Albert Museum, London / V&A Images -- All rights reserved.

Additional design by Brenda Cole, Rachel Bromley and Emily Barden

With thanks to Ruth King